12/2020

Victoria
may you learn
to reach for the
word of God, when life
bring you doubt. Speak
Pray to God, may you
always have Peace &
Love in your heart.
I love you
Sweetheart
❤ mom

PRAYERS & PROMISES
FOR
Comfort and
Encouragement

BroadStreet
PUBLISHING

CONTENTS

Introduction

Everyone experiences difficult seasons in life. Loss, pain, anxiety, and frustration can lead to discouragement and sometimes a feeling of hopelessness.

Prayers & Promises for Comfort and Encouragement is a topically organized collection that guides you through themes of assurance, compassion, inspiration, purpose, and more. Encouraging Scriptures, heartfelt prayers, and prompting questions give you an opportunity to think more deeply about the hope found in God's Word.

By staying connected to God, and believing in his promises, you can live a fulfilling, blessed life. Find your peace in his presence. Take comfort in knowing that he cares deeply for you and he will always be with you.

Ability

"My grace is sufficient for you, for my power is made perfect in weakness." Therefore I will boast all the more gladly of my weaknesses, so that the power of Christ may rest upon me.

2 Corinthians 12:9 ESV

After you have suffered for a little while, the God of all grace, who called you to His eternal glory in Christ, will Himself perfect, confirm, strengthen and establish you.

1 Peter 5:10 NASB

Take a new grip with your tired hands and strengthen your weak knees. Mark out a straight path for your feet so that those who are weak and lame will not fall but become strong.

Hebrews 12:12-13 NLT

Sometimes, Lord, I question your call on my life. I deeply desire to follow you and do great things in your name, but I don't trust my own humanity. Thank you for the numerous examples in the Bible of times you chose to use weak men and women to carry out your mission.

Thank you for the times in my life when you've used me in spite of my shortcomings. May they serve as a reminder that true strength is only found in you. Thank you for having grace with my inabilities and granting me the ability to proceed with what you have called me to do.

Do you believe that God can make
you able to do what he asks?

Acceptance

"The Father gives me the people who are mine.
Every one of them will come to me,
and I will always accept them."

JOHN 6:37 NCV

The LORD does not see as man sees; for man looks at the
outward appearance, but the LORD looks at the heart.

If God is for us, who can be against us?

ROMANS 8:31 ESV

Before he made the world, God chose us to be his very
own through what Christ would do for us; he decided
then to make us holy in his eyes, without a single fault—
we who stand before him covered with his love.

EPHESIANS 1:4 TLB

*Father, sometimes when people act wrongly toward me,
I struggle to forgive them and let the grievance go. I know
you do not hold my sins against me but receive me in my
brokenness.*

*Please give me the grace to likewise accept the imperfection
of others and treat them the way I have been treated by you.
Remind me, Lord, of the incredible price you paid for me and
also for them.*

How does God's acceptance of you help
you be more accepting of others?

Adoption

You did not receive a spirit of slavery to fall back into fear, but you have received a spirit of adoption. When we cry, "Abba! Father!" it is that very Spirit bearing witness with our spirit that we are children of God.

ROMANS 8:15–16 NRSV

A father of the fatherless and a judge for the widows,
Is God in His holy habitation.
God makes a home for the lonely;
He leads out the prisoners into prosperity.

PSALM 68:5-6 NASB

The LORD will not abandon His people on account of His great name, because the LORD has been pleased to make you a people for Himself.

1 SAMUEL 12:22 NASB

Adoption speaks of inclusion, intentionality, and newness. It baffles me, God, that you would choose me to be your child! Thank you for pulling me from my lost state and placing me in your family.

Thank you for promising to never forsake me. When I consider what you have done for me, I feel accepted, cherished, and safe.

How does knowing that God has adopted you into his family make you feel?

Affection

I am my beloved's,
And his desire is toward me.

SONG OF SOLOMON 7:10 NKJV

You make known to me the path of life;
you will fill me with joy in your presence,
with eternal pleasures at your right hand.

PSALM 16:11 NIV

My beloved speaks and says to me:
"Arise, my love, my beautiful one,
and come away,
for behold, the winter is past;
the rain is over and gone.
The flowers appear on the earth,
the time of singing has come."

SONG OF SOLOMON 2:10–12 ESV

Father, please help me cancel out the lies of the enemy which tell me I'm unlovable or need to be somebody I'm not. Your affection is hard to fathom because I struggle to see past my own depravity.

Your love, however, is not conditional of my deservedness but is an overflow of your goodness. Thank you for creating me to be the recipient of your affection.

Do you feel the affection of God in your life?

Assurance

To him who is able to do immeasurably more than all we
ask or imagine, according to his power that is at work
within us, to him be glory...for ever and ever! Amen.

EPHESIANS 3:20–21 NIV

All of God's promises have been fulfilled in Christ
with a resounding "Yes!"

2 CORINTHIANS 1:20 NLT

Jesus Christ is the same yesterday and today and forever.

HEBREWS 13:8 NASB

These things I have written to you who believe in the
name of the Son of God, that you may know that you have
eternal life, and that you may continue to believe in the
name of the Son of God.

1 JOHN 5:13 NKJV

God, when all the worries of daily life engulf me, I begin to feel overwhelmed and anxious. When I change my focus and use your Word to light my path, my vision clears and my perspective accurately adjusts.

I do not wish to use this as a reason to avoid life's problems, but I cling to the assurance that you are with me while I walk through them, each step of the way, no matter what.

How does believing God's promises
cause you to feel reassured?

Authenticity

"Remember this: If you have a lofty opinion of yourself and seek to be honored, you will be humbled. But if you have a modest opinion of yourself and choose to humble yourself, you will be honored."

MATTHEW 23:12 TPT

What should be our proper response to God's marvelous mercies? I encourage you to surrender yourselves to God to be his sacred, living sacrifices. And live in holiness, experiencing all that delights his heart. For this becomes your genuine expression of worship. Stop imitating the ideals and opinions of the culture around you, but be inwardly transformed by the Holy Spirit through a total reformation of how you think. This will empower you to discern God's will as you live a beautiful life, satisfying and perfect in his eyes.

ROMANS 12:1–2 TPT

God, I am painfully aware of the imbalance in our relationship. There have been countless times when I was unfaithful to you and you still remained devoted to me. I do not pretend to be deserving of your love and loyalty, but I accept them gratefully.

You are not impressed by lofty, religious airs, as I may fool myself into imagining. What you ask me for is worship from a contrite heart, honestly aware of my need for you. That is how I will come before you today.

How do you see yourself?
How do you think God sees you?

Blessing

Surely, LORD, you bless those who do what is right.
Like a shield, your loving care keeps them safe.

PSALM 5:12 NIRV

Surely you have granted him unending blessings
and made him glad with the joy of your presence.

PSALM 21:6 NIV

Give praise to the God and Father of our Lord Jesus
Christ. He has blessed us with every spiritual blessing.
Those blessings come from the heavenly world. They
belong to us because we belong to Christ. God chose us to
belong to Christ before the world was created. He chose
us to be holy and without blame in his eyes. He loved us.

EPHESIANS 1:3-4 NIRV

Everywhere I look, Father, I am confronted with your blessings. Some of them seem incredible, while others I have adjusted to perceiving as commonplace. The sun rises every morning and I take it for granted, yet it is one of your wonderous miracles nonetheless.

Please give me fresh eyes to recognize the countless blessings that surround me, so I may always be in awe of you and never doubt your provision and protection.

Which of God's blessings come to your mind today?

Boldness

He proclaimed the kingdom of God and taught about
the Lord Jesus Christ—with all boldness and without
hindrance!

ACTS 28:31 NIV

Sinners run away even when no one is chasing them.
But those who do what is right are as bold as lions.

PROVERBS 28:1 NIRV

On the day I called you, you answered me.
You made me strong and brave.

PSALM 138:3 NCV

Let us come boldly to the throne of our gracious God.
There we will receive his mercy,
and we will find grace to help us when we need it most.

HEBREWS 4:16 NLT

Lord, give me boldness so I can speak truth in the moments that matter. My insecurities can cause a crippling timidity to overtake me, so help me see past myself and remember that my boldness stems from the assurance I have in you.

Help me to not be intimidated by those who are stronger or smarter because you are more powerful and wise than anyone. It is on behalf of you and not myself that I step up and speak out.

Why is it sometimes hard to be bold?

Comfort

God's dwelling place is now among the people, and he will
dwell with them…. "He will wipe every tear from their
eyes. There will be no more death" or mourning or crying
or pain, for the old order of things has passed away.

REVELATION 21:3–4 NIV

May our Lord Jesus Christ himself and God our Father,
who loved us and by his grace gave us eternal comfort
and a wonderful hope, comfort you and strengthen you.

2 THESSALONIANS 2:16–17 NLT

Unless the LORD had helped me,
I would soon have settled in the silence of the grave.
I cried out, "I am slipping!"
but your unfailing love, O LORD, supported me.
When doubts filled my mind,
your comfort gave me renewed hope and cheer.

PSALM 94:17–19 NLT

Worldly comforts are, at times, so enticing. But when true comfort is required, there is no substitute for the calm serenity your Holy Spirit brings to my soul. I try to liken it to the wind and the waves, but there is no explaining it, God, there is only experiencing it.

I feel it in the worst moments of my life when you whisper to my heart, "It's going to be okay, my child, I have you."

Do you feel the comforting presence of God today?

Compassion

When I am with those who are weak, I share their
weakness, for I want to bring the weak to Christ.
Yes, I try to find common ground with everyone,
doing everything I can to save some.

1 CORINTHIANS 9:22 NLT

God, have mercy on me according to your faithful love.
Because your love is so tender and kind,
wipe out my lawless acts.

PSALM 51:1 NIRV

Praise be to the God and Father of our Lord Jesus Christ,
the Father of compassion and the God of all comfort.

2 CORINTHIANS 1:3 NIV

Father, you saw my suffering and my dejection, and you had compassion on me. You intervened on my behalf, forgave me, and remade me. Then you asked me to extend the same grace to others.

May the compassion I have been given be the overflow that I pour out on others. The realization of your love toward me will fuel my grace toward others who may at times be difficult to love. They are as much in need of compassion as I am.

How can you be a more compassionate person?

Composure

Don't worry about anything; instead, pray about
everything. Tell God what you need, and thank him for all
he has done. Then you will experience God's peace, which
exceeds anything we can understand. His peace will guard
your hearts and minds as you live in Christ Jesus.

PHILIPPIANS 4:6–7 NLT

Worry weighs a person down;
an encouraging word cheers a person up.

PROVERBS 12:25 NLT

"Which of you by worrying can add a single hour
to his life's span?"

LUKE 12:25 NASB

Give your burdens to the LORD,
and he will take care of you.

PSALM 55:22 NLT

Make me like a tree with deep roots, God. When the worries of the world weigh me down, help me maintain my composure by being firmly rooted in you.

Nothing is able to shake me when you are with me. Your Word promises that if I give you my burdens you will take care of me, so I am choosing to do that today.

How can you remain steady when it feels like your world is crumbling around you?

Confidence

I can do everything through Christ,
who gives me strength.

PHILIPPIANS 4:13 NLT

Be my rock of refuge,
to which I can always go;
give the command to save me,
for you are my rock and my fortress....
For you have been my hope, Sovereign LORD,
my confidence since my youth.

PSALM 71:3, 5 NIV

Do not throw away your confidence,
which has a great reward.

HEBREWS 10:35 NCV

God, your Word assures me that through you, I can do everything, yet so often my confidence wavers. Every challenge I have encountered, you have led me though. Your promise to me of being my hope and my confidence will never fail.

Please help me to recall these times of victory when I feel overwhelmed or insecure so I can have confidence knowing that you are with me always.

How do you find your confidence?

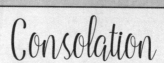

Consolation

You, O LORD, are a shield about me,
My glory, and the One who lifts my head.

PSALM 3:3 NASB

Blessed be the LORD,
Because He has heard the voice of my supplication.
The LORD is my strength and my shield;
My heart trusts in Him, and I am helped;
Therefore my heart exults,
And with my song I shall thank Him.

PSALM 28:6-7 NASB

Those that the LORD has rescued will return.
They will enter Zion with singing;
everlasting joy will crown their heads.
Gladness and joy will overtake them,
and sorrow and sighing will flee away.

ISAIAH 35:10 NIV

*In the darkest moments when words no longer comfort,
your peace calms and encourages me. Your consolation
can carry me through the worst of times when everything
else falls short.*

Thank you for being my strength and my shield, God.

How do you feel you have been consoled by God in your moments of grief?

Contentment

To enjoy your work and to accept your lot in life—that is
indeed a gift from God. The person who does that will
not need to look back with sorrow on his past, for God
gives him joy.

ECCLESIASTES 5:20 TLB

I know what it is to be in need, and I know what it is to
have plenty. I have learned the secret of being content
in any and every situation, whether well fed or hungry,
whether living in plenty or in want. I can do all this
through him who gives me strength.

PHILIPPIANS 4:12-13 NIV

God, I understand that the purpose of this season is not just to transition me into the next season. Regardless of what is coming or what I'm aiming at, you have a purpose for today.

You have lessons you want to teach me and blessings you want to give me now. Please help me grow in contentment and appreciate what you have already done in my life.

How can you choose to be content
with your life as it is right now?

Courage

Be strong in the Lord and in his mighty power. Put on the
full armor of God, so that you can take your stand against
the devil's schemes.

EPHESIANS 6:10-11 NIV

Be alert. Continue strong in the faith.
Have courage, and be strong. Do everything in love.

1 CORINTHIANS 16:13-14 NCV

Even though I walk through the darkest valley,
I will not be afraid. You are with me.
Your shepherd's rod and staff comfort me.

PSALM 23:4 NIRV

"This is my command—be strong and courageous!
Do not be afraid or discouraged.
For the LORD your God is with you wherever you go."

JOSHUA 1:9 NLT

Wherever I go, Father, you promise you'll be there. That means whatever I face I won't face alone because you are always with me.

Please grant me courage to walk through everything that comes my way, knowing that you have already equipped me with all that I need to live a life of godliness and unrelenting faith.

When was the last time you asked
God for courage?

Delight

When I received your words, I ate them.
They filled me with joy. My heart took delight in them.
Lord God who rules over all, I belong to you.

JEREMIAH 15:16 NIRV

"My God, I want to do what you want.
Your teachings are in my heart."

PSALM 40:8 NCV

Your laws are my treasure;
they are my heart's delight.

PSALM 119:111 NLT

"Let your light shine before others, that they may see
your good deeds and glorify your Father in heaven."

MATTHEW 5:16 NIV

It confounds me, dear God, that you delight in me as much as your Word expresses. You call me your beloved and friend. When I forget this truth, you remind me. You sent your Son to demonstrate how much you love us, and your Word reaffirms it over and over.

Furthermore, I delight in you! Your Word brings me limitless joy and the time we spend together is unparalleled in importance to me.

How hard is it for you to fathom
God's incredible delight in you?

Deliverance

Humble yourselves in the sight of the Lord,
and He will lift you up.

JAMES 4:10 NKJV

My prayer is to you, O LORD.
At an acceptable time, O God,
in the abundance of your steadfast love
answer me in your saving faithfulness.
Deliver me from sinking in the mire;
let me be delivered from my enemies
and from the deep waters.
Answer me, O LORD, for your steadfast love is good;
according to your abundant mercy, turn to me.

PSALM 69:13-14, 16 ESV

The righteous person faces many troubles,
but the LORD comes to the rescue each time.

PSALM 34:19 NLT

God, you did not promise that I would be free from misfortune. In fact, your Word reveals that a righteous person is guaranteed to encounter trouble. Your promise to me is that you will come to my rescue and deliver me.

Please deliver me from my fears today. I am not asking for an easy life or that you remove all problems from my path, but that you give me confidence in knowing that there is no trial so great that you won't deliver me from it.

Can you ask God for deliverance
from your fears?

Devotion

Commit everything you do to the LORD.
Trust him, and he will help you.

PSALM 37:5 NLT

With all my heart I have sought You;
Do not let me wander from Your commandments.
Your word I have treasured in my heart,
That I may not sin against You.

PSALM 119:10–11 NASB

"If any of you wants to be my follower, you must turn
from your selfish ways, take up your cross daily,
and follow me."

LUKE 9:23 NLT

"Seek first the kingdom of God and His righteousness,
and all these things shall be added to you."

MATTHEW 6:33 NKJV

Nothing is able to stand between you and me, Father God. Your devotion to me is unrelenting. You are always faithful to help me in my weakness. I want to express my devotion to you as well, and daily take up my cross to follow you.

I will read your Word and hide it in my heart so I clearly know what you have asked of me and will not sin against you. Thank you for your love and devotion to me.

Can you sense God's absolute
devotion toward you?

Encouragement

The LORD your God is with you;
the mighty One will save you.
He will rejoice over you. You will rest in his love;
he will sing and be joyful about you.

ZEPHANIAH 3:17 NCV

Nothing is more appealing than speaking beautiful,
life-giving words.
For they release sweetness to our souls
and inner healing to our spirits.

PROVERBS 16:24 TPT

Be joyful. Grow to maturity. Encourage each other.
Live in harmony and peace.
Then the God of love and peace will be with you.

2 CORINTHIANS 13:11 NLT

God, you told us that when we gather together in your name, you are with us. You said that when we encourage each other and live in harmony, you will be there. You are a God of peace, love, and joy!

Show me ways today to extend that peace, love, and joy to others and be an encouragement to them. This, you tell me, will refresh my soul and bring health to my body. The way you created me to need others is masterfully designed. Thank you for your encouragement and for others who have encouraged me.

How can you encourage someone today?

Enrichment

Oh, the depth of the riches both of the wisdom
and knowledge of God!
How unsearchable are His judgments
and unfathomable His ways!

ROMANS 11:33 NASB

Blessed are those who find wisdom,
those who gain understanding,
for she is more profitable than silver
and yields better returns than gold.
She is more precious than rubies;
nothing you desire can compare with her.
Long life is in her right hand;
in her left hand are riches and honor.
Her ways are pleasant ways,
and all her paths are peace.

PROVERBS 3:13–17 NIV

True wealth and profit can only be found in knowing you and in the wisdom you give. My relationship with you is so precious and has enriched my life in ways no worldly goods could.

I will seek your wisdom with a greater desire than if I were searching for the most precious stones because I know that every good gift comes from you. Thank you for filling my life with blessings and eternal riches.

How has God enriched your life lately?

Eternity

We are citizens of heaven,
where the Lord Jesus Christ lives.
And we are eagerly waiting for him
to return as our Savior.

PHILIPPIANS 3:20 NLT

That will happen in a flash, as quickly as you can wink an
eye. It will happen at the blast of the last trumpet. Then the
dead will be raised to live forever. And we will be changed.

1 CORINTHIANS 15:52 NIRV

Why would I fear the future? For your goodness and love
pursue me all the days of my life. Then afterward, when
my life is through, I'll return to your glorious presence to
be forever with you!

PSALM 23:6 TPT

I do not live for this life but for the hope of an eternal home with you. God, although I want to live intentionally and offer praise to you here on earth, I know that I was created for your kingdom and not simply this temporal existence.

My treasures are not here, they are with you. My hopes and dreams are not wasted on present passing idols, they are focused forward to that "flash of an eye" when you come back for me.

Can you view eternity with a hopeful, happy heart, fully trusting in a good God?

Faith

Through Christ you have come to trust in God. And you
have placed your faith and hope in God because he raised
Christ from the dead and gave him great glory.

1 Peter 1:21 NLT

"If you have faith as small as a mustard seed, it is enough.
You can say to this mountain, 'Move from here to there.'
And it will move. Nothing will be impossible for you."

Matthew 17:20 NIRV

The important thing is faith—
the kind of faith that works through love.

Galatians 5:6 NCV

Faith is confidence in what we hope for
and assurance about what we do not see.

Hebrews 11:1 NIV

*Since the beginning of time you have proven your faithfulness
to us, Father. Your goodness has never wavered and your
character is unchanged. I can confidently put my faith in you
because you have always been and always will be faithful
and true.*

*Even when I waver, what little faith I can offer you still accept
and can use to move mountains. Even though I can't see
what's coming, I know I can trust you.*

What gives you faith and hope in Jesus?

Faithfulness

Your lovingkindness, O LORD, extends to the heavens,
Your faithfulness reaches to the skies.

PSALM 36:5 NASB

The Lord is faithful, who will establish you
and guard you from the evil one.

2 THESSALONIANS 3:3 NKJV

LORD, you are my God; I will exalt you and praise
your name, for in perfect faithfulness you have done
wonderful things, things planned long ago.

ISAIAH 25:1 NIV

The word of the LORD is upright,
and all his work is done in faithfulness.

PSALM 33:4 ESV

Your faithfulness is what has established me. At times, I can become so distracted by where I'd like to be that I fail to realize how far you have already brought me.

You have protected me from evil, released me from my sin, anointed me as your heir, reserved for me a place in heaven with you, and always remained true to your promises. Thank you.

How have you seen the faithfulness
of God played out in your life?

Fear

God gave us his Spirit. And the Spirit doesn't make us
weak and fearful. Instead, the Spirit gives us power and
love. He helps us control ourselves.

2 TIMOTHY 1:7 NIRV

The LORD is my light and my salvation—
whom shall I fear?
The LORD is the stronghold of my life—
of whom shall I be afraid?

PSALM 27:1 NIV

When I am afraid, I will trust you.
I praise God for his word.
I trust God, so I am not afraid.
What can human beings do to me?

PSALM 56:3-4 NCV

The damage others are able to inflict on me is severely limited because, God, you hold my heart. You are my light, my salvation, and the stronghold of my life. You are my helper and you equip me with confidence to overcome my fears.

Each and every fear I have, even the most hidden ones, you are aware of and will give me the tenacity to face them with power and in love.

What fears can you give to God right now?

Forgiveness

He is so rich in kindness and grace that he purchased our
freedom with the blood of his Son and forgave our sins.

EPHESIANS 1:7 NLT

As far as the east is from the west,
So far has He removed our transgressions from us.

PSALM 103:12 NASB

If we confess our sins, He is faithful and just to forgive us
our sins and to cleanse us from all unrighteousness.

1 JOHN 1:9 NKJV

"Her sins—and they are many—have been forgiven,
so she has shown me much love. But a person who is
forgiven little shows only little love."

LUKE 7:47 NLT

Father, I ask that you help me forgive those who have done me wrong. It is not a matter of whether or not they deserve forgiveness, I want to extend it because I was also guilty and you forgave me. My aim is to be like you!

Please walk me through releasing my desire for justice to you, knowing that you are a just and loving God. You understand each situation far better than I could, and I can trust you to make all things right. Thank you for not holding my sins against me. Your forgiveness allows me to forgive others.

Is there someone who needs your forgiveness today?

Freedom

The Lord is the Spirit,
and where the Spirit of the Lord is,
there is freedom.

2 CORINTHIANS 3:17 NIV

Beloved ones, God has called us to live a life of freedom
in the Holy Spirit. But don't view this wonderful freedom
as an opportunity to set up a base of operations in the
natural realm. Freedom means that we become so
completely free of self-indulgence that we become
servants of one another, expressing love in all we do.

GALATIANS 5:13 TPT

We have freedom now, because Christ made us free.
So stand strong. Do not change and go back into the
slavery of the law.

GALATIANS 5:1 NCV

The difference between me and someone who is unsaved is the freedom I now live in because I accepted your forgiveness. I want to use this liberty to help others who are still trapped in bondage. I want them to understand that it is not on account of my merit that I walk in freedom, but only by your grace. This same grace you extend to them.

The forgiveness I have been given drives me to do good, not for the notion that I could ever earn or repay your goodness, but as an outpouring of the gratefulness I feel each day as I walk in freedom.

How does it feel to be free from your sin?

Friendship

A friend loves you all the time,
and a brother helps in time of trouble.

PROVERBS 17:17 NCV

There are "friends" who destroy each other,
but a real friend sticks closer than a brother.

PROVERBS 18:24 NLT

"Greater love has no one than this: to lay down one's
life for one's friends. You are my friends if you do what
I command.... Instead, I have called you friends, for
everything that I learned from my Father I have made
known to you."

JOHN 15:13-15 NIV

"In everything, do to others what you would want them
to do to you."

MATTHEW 7:12 NIRV

There is nothing you wouldn't do for your friends, Lord. You modeled what true friendship looks like, and then lovingly instructed me to go and do likewise. Real, selfless friendship is not easy, but I have your example to follow. Thank you for the friends you have given me and the love they have shown me.

Thank you for the ones who still stand with me through the hard times. Thank you for the people in my life who don't just tell me what I want to hear, but encourage me to continue drawing nearer to you.

What friends spur you on in your relationship with God?

Goodness

Everything God created is good, and nothing is to be
rejected if it is received with thanksgiving.

1 Timothy 4:4 NIV

Taste and see that the LORD is good.
Oh, the joys of those who take refuge in him!

Psalm 34:8 NLT

My brothers and sisters, I am sure that you are full of
goodness. I know that you have all the knowledge you
need and that you are able to teach each other.

Romans 15:14 NCV

How can I begin to comprehend your goodness, God? Everywhere I look I see your hand at work in my life. You are my Creator, Savior, and sustainer. You provide a refuge for me to be safe. You offer forgiveness from sin through your sacrifice, so I am pure enough to draw near to you.

You designed me for an eternal kingdom while still providing for all my earthly needs. I can only just begin to recognize the ways your goodness has reformed my life.

Where do you see the goodness of God the most in your life?

Grace

From his fullness we have all received,
grace upon grace.

JOHN 1:16 NRSV

God gives us even more grace,
as the Scripture says,
"God is against the proud,
but he gives grace to the humble."

JAMES 4:6 NCV

Remember this: sin will not conquer you,
for God already has! You are not governed by law
but governed by the reign of the grace of God.

ROMANS 6:14 TPT

Having been removed from the bondage of the law by your grace, I can now obey your commandments from a heart of love and gratitude, rather than as the joyless obligation of a servant. Your grace is my freedom. In humility, I will accept your grace and follow you every day of my life.

I will enjoy our friendship, learn from your teachings, extend grace to others, and one day enter your kingdom. All these things I can do because, by your grace, I am your child and not merely a servant.

What does God's grace look like in your life?

Grief

Those who sow in tears shall reap with shouts of joy.

Let your steadfast love become my comfort
according to your promise to your servant.

"Come to me, all you who are weary and burdened,
and I will give you rest. Take my yoke upon you and learn
from me, for I am gentle and humble in heart,
and you will find rest for your souls."

Every valley shall be raised up,
every mountain and hill made low;
the rough ground shall become level,
the rugged places a plain.

I have experienced times of terrible grief, but you have always been faithful to walk with me through them. You are no stranger to grief, Father, and you console me like nothing else can. Furthermore, you have overcome grief. It is temporary and you are everlasting.

There is coming a day when sorrow will end and there will be no more tears. Until that day comes, please continue to comfort me and allow me to lean on you for strength.

Do you ask God for help when you need his comfort?

Guidance

Guide me in your truth and teach me,
for you are God my Savior,
and my hope is in you all day long.

PSALM 25:5 NIV

Wise people can also listen and learn;
even they can find good advice in these words.

PROVERBS 1:5 NCV

We can make our plans,
but the LORD determines our steps.

PROVERBS 16:9 NLT

Those who are led by the Spirit of God
are children of God.

ROMANS 8:14 NIRV

God, sometimes I get irritated when things don't go the way I plan. You are the One directing my steps, and that knowledge gives me peace that supersedes the disruptions. You determine my path. I want to be led by your Spirit.

Guide me in your ways and grant me wisdom to listen and learn. Do not allow me to become so stuck in my ways that I lose sight of your guidance.

Is there anything God can help
guide you in today?

Health

The world and its desires pass away,
but whoever does the will of God lives forever.

1 JOHN 2:17 NIV

Don't think for a moment that you know it all, for
wisdom comes when you adore him with undivided
devotion and avoid everything that's wrong.
Then you will find the healing refreshment your body
and spirit long for.

PROVERBS 3:7-8 TPT

I will never forget your commandments,
for by them you give me life.

PSALM 119:93 NLT

A happy heart is like good medicine,
but a broken spirit drains your strength.

PROVERBS 17:22 NCV

You are a masterful designer, God, and you created our bodies to need you in order to truly thrive. Your Word says that respecting you and obeying your commandments will help me experience health and strength. A joyful disposition not only uplifts me emotionally, but it also brings wellness to my physical body.

Thank you, Lord, for the ways you have provided for me both physically and emotionally. Thank you for the joy and the health you have given me. Thank you that in the end I know everything will be made new.

What healing are you believing God for right now?

Hope

The LORD is good to those whose hope is in him,
to the one who seeks him.

LAMENTATIONS 3:25 NIV

Hope will never bring us shame. That's because God's
love has poured into our hearts. This happened through
the Holy Spirit, who has been given to us.

ROMANS 5:5 NIRV

The LORD's delight is in those who fear him,
those who put their hope in his unfailing love.

PSALM 147:11 NLT

Father, I can hope in things unseen because I know that I am seen. You see me, listen to me, and love me. Because you are good, I can put my hope in you and seek you with all my heart. You have given me your Spirit and poured out your love on me.

I have assurance that my hope will never be put to shame. Because your delight is in me, I hope for all your promises and have confidence in them because your love for me never fails.

Knowing that God always hears you,
what can you be hopeful for?

Inspiration

The precepts of the LORD are right,
giving joy to the heart.
The commands of the LORD are radiant,
giving light to the eyes.

PSALM 19:8 NIV

Your laws are my treasure;
they are my heart's delight.

PSALM 119:111 NLT

The whole Bible was given to us by inspiration from
God and is useful to teach us what is true and to make us
realize what is wrong in our lives; it straightens us out
and helps us do what is right.

2 TIMOTHY 3:16 TLB

Father, you inspire me by your life, your Word, and your creation. When I spend time with you, I am inspired to love deeper and with more abandon. Reading the Scriptures encourages me to press forward toward my goal of knowing you more.

Everywhere I look I am surrounded by testimonies of your beauty and creativity which makes me want to pursue truth and uncover your treasures. You inspire me to see things the way you do.

How do you find inspiration?

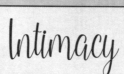

Intimacy

O LORD, You have searched me and known me.
You know my sitting down and my rising up;
You understand my thought afar off.
You comprehend my path and my lying down,
And are acquainted with all my ways.
For there is not a word on my tongue,
But behold, O LORD, You know it altogether.

PSALM 139:1–4, NKJV

All that I know now is partial and incomplete,
but then I will know everything completely,
just as God now knows me completely.

1 CORINTHIANS 13:12 NLT

God's solid foundation stands firm, sealed with this
inscription: "The Lord knows those who are his."

2 TIMOTHY 2:19 NIV

I long for intimacy with you, God, but what is truly astounding is you long for it with me! You desire me so much that you came to earth and paid for my sins so I could be with you. There is so much you want to share with me, I can only imagine the joy you have when I share what little I have with you.

Please take all of me—whatever I have to offer you. Everything I am and have is because of you. I love you.

How does being truly known by God encourage you?

Joy

May the God of hope fill you with all joy and peace as you
trust in him, so that you may overflow with hope by the
power of the Holy Spirit.

ROMANS 15:13 NIV

"Don't be sad, because the joy of the LORD
will make you strong."

NEHEMIAH 8:10 NCV

The LORD is my strength and shield.
I trust him with all my heart.
He helps me, and my heart is filled with joy.
I burst out in songs of thanksgiving.

PSALM 28:7 NLT

Always be joyful because you belong to the Lord.
I will say it again. Be joyful!

PHILIPPIANS 4:4 NIRV

Your joy is more than mere happiness, Lord, it is everlasting sustenance. Joy that comes from you fills me with peace, strength, and thankfulness. It is not a moment of fleeting satisfaction, but an enduring force that sustains me regardless of my circumstances.

God, I am so grateful that your joy is not dependent on my situation like worldly pleasures are, but is a gift that you freely give to those who fear and follow you.

What is one truly joyful moment you've had recently?

Justice

He will not break the bruised reed, nor quench the dimly burning flame. He will encourage the fainthearted, those tempted to despair. He will see full justice given to all who have been wronged.

ISAIAH 42:3 TLB

Beloved, do not avenge yourselves,
but rather give place to wrath; for it is written,
"Vengeance is Mine, I will repay," says the Lord.

ROMANS 12:19 NKJV

He will not judge by appearance, false evidence,
or hearsay, but will defend the poor and the exploited.
He will rule against the wicked who oppress them.
For he will be clothed with fairness and with truth.

ISAIAH 11:3–5 TLB

The wrongs of this world can seem overwhelming and I yearn for your justice, God. Help me to trust your omniscience and your justice. You are the Judge and not me. Your justice is perfectly executed, coupled with your mercy. Mine is flawed and biased. I can forgive and move on.

Today, I will not seek vengeance for myself, but will submit everything to you and follow your example. You are more aware than anyone of the condition of the world, and you have a perfect plan in place.

Can you leave justice in God's hands?

Kindness

Be kind to each other, tenderhearted, forgiving one
another, just as God through Christ has forgiven you.

EPHESIANS 4:32 NLT

Kind people do themselves a favor,
but cruel people bring trouble on themselves.

PROVERBS 11:17 NCV

Do you disrespect God's great kindness and favor?
Do you disrespect God when he is patient with you?
Don't you realize that God's kindness is meant
to turn you away from your sins?

ROMANS 2:4 NIRV

For great is his love toward us,
and the faithfulness of the LORD endures forever.
Praise the LORD.

PSALM 117:2 NIV

Father, you have asked us to be kind to each other and forgive offenses. Not only is this for your glory, but also for my own welfare. Your Word warns me that cruelty invites trouble but by extending kindness I do myself a favor.

Furthermore, you chose to show me kindness and forgiveness, so what right do I have to withhold the same treatment from others? That would be disrespectful to you and a disservice to myself and my testimony. Help me recognize the eternal importance of simply acting kind.

How can you extend kindness to those around you today?

Life

All praise to God, the Father of our Lord Jesus Christ.
It is by his great mercy that we have been born again,
because God raised Jesus Christ from the dead. Now we
live with great expectation.

1 Peter 1:3 NLT

That faith and that knowledge come from the hope for life
forever, which God promised to us before time began.

Titus 1:2 NCV

"I am the way and the truth and the life.
No one comes to the Father except through me."

John 14:6 NIRV

You gave me life. Then, you saved my life with your own blood. As if that were not miraculous enough, you gave my life meaning and a purpose. You have richly blessed me and have offered me eternal life.

I don't want to squander this gift or your sacrifice. Rather, I want to live my life to the fullest extent and bring you glory. Please guide me when I am confronted with big opportunities and also in the mundane day-to-day tasks so my whole life brings you praise.

What is your favorite part of life?

Loneliness

"Teach them to obey everything that I have taught you,
and I will be with you always,
even until the end of this age."

MATTHEW 28:20 NCV

The LORD is near to all who call on him,
yes, to all who call on him in truth.

PSALM 145:18 NLT

Even if my father and mother abandon me,
the LORD will hold me close.

PSALM 27:10 NLT

"Be strong and courageous. Do not be afraid or terrified
because of them, for the LORD your God goes with you;
he will never leave you nor forsake you."

DEUTERONOMY 31:6 NIV

There is nowhere I can go that you will not go with me. You promise to always be near me and to answer when I call to you. Even if my own parents or my closest friends were to abandon me, you never will.

You have broken through the clutch loneliness had on my life and have become my best friend. Thank you for surrounding me with your presence and walking with me each step of the way.

When you feel lonely, can you turn
to God and ask him to surround you
with his presence?

Loss

Those who sow in tears shall reap with shouts of joy.

PSALM 126:5 ESV

Let your steadfast love become my comfort
according to your promise to your servant.

PSALM 119:76 NRSV

Every valley shall be raised up, every mountain and hill
made low; the rough ground shall become level,
the rugged places a plain.

ISAIAH 40:4 NIV

The earth may fall apart. The mountains may fall into the
middle of the sea. But we will not be afraid. The waters
of the sea may roar and foam. The mountains may shake
when the waters rise. But we will not be afraid. God's
blessings are like a river. They fill the city of God with joy.

PSALM 46:2-4 NIRV

God, in my life I have endured times of immense loss, but that is not where my story ends. You do not leave me in the valley. I will rise again and, leaning on you, make my way up to the mountain top. It's steep and I stumble at times, but I know I cannot sit in the empty feeling of loss forever.

There is too much that you want to give me for me to fixate on what has been taken. You are my worth—the One who fills my empty cup.

Do you ask God for help when you need his comfort?

Love

Three things will last forever—
faith, hope, and love—
and the greatest of these is love.

1 CORINTHIANS 13:13 NLT

LORD, you are good. You are forgiving.
You are full of love for all who call out to you.

PSALM 86:5 NIRV

Fill us with your love every morning.
Then we will sing and rejoice all our lives.

PSALM 90:14 NCV

Let love and faithfulness never leave you;
bind them around your neck,
write them on the tablet of your heart.

PROVERBS 3:3 NIV

Your love, Lord, is everlasting! It is superior to faith, hope, and even the tongues of men and angels. Fill me with your love every morning so I can spend every day praising you and loving others.

Your love gives me strength, puts joy in my heart, and casts out my fears. I want to share it with everyone I know.

How does the love of God in your life help you to love others?

Patience

Warn those who are lazy.
Encourage those who are timid.
Take tender care of those who are weak.
Be patient with everyone.

1 Thessalonians 5:14 NLT

Be like those who through faith and patience
will receive what God has promised.

Hebrews 6:12 NCV

Be completely humble and gentle;
be patient, bearing with one another in love.

Ephesians 4:2 NIV

Anyone who is patient has great understanding.
But anyone who gets angry quickly
shows how foolish they are.

Proverbs 14:29 NIRV

Patience can teach me many things, God. In fact, you tell me that I receive your promises by way of my faith and through exercising patience. Alternatively, when I act in hasty anger and am easily set off, I show everyone that I am foolish.

I cannot see what you see, and I do not always understand what people are going through. It is best to listen to what you have said and have patience with everyone.

How can you show more patience in your life?

Peace

"I have told you these things, so that you can have peace
because of me. In this world you will have trouble.
But be encouraged! I have won the battle over the world."

JOHN 16:33 NIRV

The LORD gives his people strength.
The LORD blesses them with peace.

PSALM 29:11 NLT

May the Lord himself, the Lord of peace, pour into you
his peace in every circumstance and in every possible
way. The Lord's tangible presence be with you all.

2 THESSALONIANS 3:16 TPT

"I am leaving you with a gift—peace of mind and heart.
And the peace I give is a gift the world cannot give.
So don't be troubled or afraid."

JOHN 14:27 NLT

Father, in a world filled with turmoil and uncertainty, you offer peace. This true and prevailing peace can only be found in you. The world does not possess it and cannot offer it. I cannot earn it or learn it. It is a gift and I can only choose to receive it.

Your peace is far greater than the world's troubles because you are far greater than the world. Thank you for leaving me your peace so I don't need to live in fear or confusion anymore.

What does peace look like for you?

Perseverance

In a race all the runners run.
But only one gets the prize.
You know that, don't you?
So run in a way that will get you the prize.

1 CORINTHIANS 9:24-25 NIRV

I have tried hard to find you—
don't let me wander from your commands.

PSALM 119:10 NLT

I have fought the good fight,
I have finished the race,
I have kept the faith.

2 TIMOTHY 4:7 NCV

Let us not become weary in doing good, for at the proper
time we will reap a harvest if we do not give up.

GALATIANS 6:9 NIV

God, when Moses' arms were tired, you sent others to hold them up. Through his obedience, you granted the army victory. At times, I feel so exhausted, but I know that you are holding me and helping me persevere. You have sent others to help me along and I know that I do not need to fight alone.

Doing good often requires the harder path, but it is the road I am committed to taking. I will persevere in this race because I find my rest and my refreshment in you. In faith, I will run and not lose heart.

What do you feel God is calling you to persevere in right now?

Praise

Sing to the LORD a new song,

his praise from the ends of the earth,

you who go down to the sea, and all that is in it,

you islands, and all who live in them.

ISAIAH 42:10 NIV

Praise the LORD from the skies.

Praise him high above the earth.

Praise him, all you angels.

Praise him, all you armies of heaven.

Praise him, sun and moon.

Praise him, all you shining stars.

Praise him, highest heavens

and you waters above the sky.

Let them praise the LORD,

because they were created by his command.

PSALM 148:1-5 NCV

God, I praise you because of how wonderful and powerful you are. You made me in your image and saved my life from the pit of death. You are worthy of all praise and I will never stop being amazed by all the glorious things you have done in my life.

I will not make my life about me because that is an empty existence. You give me purpose and fullness, and I will praise you for that today and every day. Thank you for the opportunity to approach you in worship because it was what I was created to do.

What is something specific you can
praise God for today?

Prayer

LORD, in the morning you hear my voice.
In the morning I pray to you.
I wait for you in hope.

PSALM 5:3 NIRV

Never stop praying.

1 THESSALONIANS 5:17 NIRV

The LORD does not listen to the wicked,
but he hears the prayers of those who do right.

PROVERBS 15:29 NCV

Come, let us bow down in worship,
let us kneel before the LORD our Maker.

PSALM 95:6 NIV

I love coming to you in prayer, Father! It astounds me that I can speak to you and you listen. Please listen to my prayers today as I recognize your greatness, thank you for your blessings, and ask you for your help.

Through prayer, I can worship you, my Creator. Through prayer, I can acknowledge the mighty things you have done in my life. Through prayer I can bring you all my tears and requests. I never want to stop praying, God.

What can you pray about right now?

Promises

His divine power has granted to us everything pertaining
to life and godliness, through the true knowledge of Him
who called us by His own glory and excellence.

2 Peter 1:3-4 nasb

Your promises have been thoroughly tested,
and your servant loves them.
My eyes stay open through the watches of the night,
that I may meditate on your promises.

Psalm 119:140, 148 niv

The Lord always keeps his promises;
he is gracious in all he does.

Psalm 145:13 nlt

All the promises of God in Him are Yes, and in Him
Amen, to the glory of God through us.

2 Corinthians 1:20 nkjv

If it weren't for your promises, I would be too weak to endure until the end. You offer strength through your promises of help and restoration for the journey now, and for relief from all grief and an eternity with you in the end. You do not require blind obedience, but have a history of fulfilled promises as far back as history dates.

You have revealed your promises for the end of the age as well and have not hidden it from me. I only need to trust you and your promises.

Which promises of God help you see hope in your current situation?

Protection

My God is my rock. I can run to him for safety. He is
my shield and my saving strength, my defender and my
place of safety. The Lord saves me from those who want
to harm me.

2 Samuel 22:3 ncv

The Lord is good, a refuge in times of trouble.
He cares for those who trust in him.

Nahum 1:7 niv

Though we experience every kind of pressure, we're not
crushed. At times we don't know what to do, but quitting
is not an option. We are persecuted by others, but God has
not forsaken us. We may be knocked down, but not out.

2 Corinthians 4:8-9 tpt

God, there is no force as mighty as you. I know that I can surrender myself to your caring and capable hands. I do not need to anguish over self-protection because if you are for me there is nothing that can come against me.

You are the God of the miraculous and you have always protected your children. There is nothing I need to be afraid of. Like a good parent, your protection covers me from every kind of evil.

How hard is it for you to lay down your battle plan and let God be your protector?

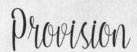

Provision

All scripture is inspired by God and is useful for teaching, for reproof, for correction, and for training in righteousness, so that everyone who belongs to God may be proficient, equipped for every good work.

2 TIMOTHY 3:16–17 NRSV

May he give you the power to accomplish all the good things your faith prompts you to do.

2 THESSALONIANS 1:11 NLT

We are God's handiwork, created in Christ Jesus to do good works, which God prepared in advance for us to do.

EPHESIANS 2:10 NIV

The LORD reached out his hand a
nd touched my mouth and said to me,
"I have put my words in your mouth."

JEREMIAH 1:9 NIV

God, there is nothing that you have called me to that you won't also provide for. At times, the task of following you can seem too difficult and I feel like I am lacking in crucial areas. However, then I remember your promises to provide for everything I need to follow you.

Your perfect provision includes the wisdom, compassion, and resources necessary for the calling you have placed on my life.

How have you seen God provide for you lately?

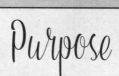

Purpose

You have been raised up with Christ.
So think about things that are in heaven.
That is where Christ is.
He is sitting at God's right hand.

COLOSSIANS 3:1 NIRV

We know that in all things God works
for the good of those who love him,
who have been called according to his purpose.

ROMANS 8:28 NIV

My child, pay attention to my words;
listen closely to what I say.
Don't ever forget my words;
keep them always in mind.

PROVERBS 4:20-21 NCV

I am in awe and humbled when I think of how you created me for a special purpose within your universal plan. Thank you for the opportunity to follow you and serve you—to fulfill the purpose you've placed on my life.

Thank you for raising me up with Christ, from death into life, for a role in your kingdom, and for sonship rather than servanthood.

How do you feel when you think about God having a special purpose for your life?

Reconciliation

We are made right with God by placing our faith in
Jesus Christ. And this is true for everyone who believes,
no matter who we are. For everyone has sinned; we
all fall short of God's glorious standard. Yet God, with
undeserved kindness, declares that we are righteous. He
did this through Christ Jesus when he freed us from the
penalty for our sins.

ROMANS 3:22–24 NLT

You were separate from Christ...foreigners to the
covenants of the promise, without hope and without God
in the world. But now in Christ Jesus you who once were
far away have been brought near by the blood of Christ.

EPHESIANS 2:12–13 NIV

Father, my sin used to separate me from you, but you reconciled our broken relationship by paying the price for my sin and reclaiming me from the grip of death. In you, I have been made new, and this complete reconciliation has secured me a place in your family.

I want to play an integral part in the lives of others and help them also reconcile their relationships with you. Show me how to use this gift for others.

Can you believe God for reconciliation
in your relationships?

Refreshment

The law of the LORD is perfect,
refreshing the soul.
The statutes of the LORD are trustworthy,
making wise the simple.

PSALM 19:7 NIV

How priceless is your unfailing love, O God!
People take refuge in the shadow of your wings.
They feast on the abundance of your house;
you give them drink from your river of delights.
For with you is the fountain of life;
in your light we see light.

PSALM 36:7–9 NIV

A generous person will prosper;
whoever refreshes others will be refreshed.

PROVERBS 11: 25 NIV

Even water cannot bring the sort of satisfaction that you do, God. Your generosity and unfailing love refresh my soul and delight my heart! Whenever I am weak or burdened, you welcome me with open arms. You give me refuge, rest, and refreshment.

Unlike water, coffee, food, or anything else I look for to refresh and nourish me here on earth, what you offer me lasts forever. It doesn't need to be replenished because it doesn't wear off or fade away. Sustain me, Lord, with your everlasting life.

In what ways do you feel refreshed by God?

Relaxation

Blessed is the one who trusts in the LORD,
whose confidence is in him.
They will be like a tree planted by the water
that sends out its roots by the stream.
It does not fear when heat comes;
its leaves are always green.
It has no worries in a year of drought
and never fails to bear fruit.

JEREMIAH 17:7–8 NIV

"Those who love me, I will deliver;
I will protect those who know my name.
When they call to me, I will answer them;
I will be with them in trouble,
I will rescue them and honor them."

PSALM 91:14-15 NRSV

Father, it can be difficult for me to relax and unwind at times. Life seems so hectic and I struggle to find spare time to sit with you and be at peace in your company. Even though you promise rest for the weary, I often overlook your offer and attempt to find my own way through this maze called life.

Please remind me to trust you and to believe that you will take care of me. Help me look to you first for the relaxation that I need every day and to make it a priority in my life.

How can you practice relaxing in God's presence?

Relief

"I am the Alpha and the Omega—the Beginning and the
End. To all who are thirsty I will give freely from the
springs of the water of life."

REVELATION 21:6 NLT

I prayed to the LORD, and he answered me.
He freed me from all my fears.
Those who look to him for help will be radiant with joy.

PSALM 34:4–5 NLT

The Spirit helps us in our weakness. We do not know
what we ought to pray for, but the Spirit himself
intercedes for us through wordless groans. And he
who searches our hearts knows the mind of the Spirit,
because the Spirit intercedes for God's people in
accordance with the will of God.

ROMANS 8:26–27 NIV

God, my soul is so anxious because of the burdens I choose to carry, but you extend rest and relief to me. Let me learn from you, Lord, and take up your yoke because you are gentle and humble.

You answer my prayers, release me from fear, and fill me with joy. Your relief is like a fresh spring that lifts my spirit and calms my anxious mind.

What relief do you need from God in your current situation?

Restoration

He has saved us and called us to a holy life—
not because of anything we have done
but because of his own purpose and grace.

2 TIMOTHY 1:9 NIV

Since we have been made right in God's sight by faith,
we have peace with God because of what Jesus Christ our
Lord has done for us. Because of our faith, Christ has
brought us into this place of undeserved privilege where
we now stand, and we confidently and joyfully look
forward to sharing God's glory.

ROMANS 5:1—2 NLT

"Let us praise the Lord, the God of Israel,
because he has come to help his people
and has given them freedom.
He has given us a powerful Savior."

LUKE 1:68-69 NCV

Since you paid for my sins with your own life, my life has been restored. You saved me because I could not save myself. You took what was dead and filled me with joy, peace, love, purpose, and bravery.

The restoration powers of your grace have set me free to walk right up to you and into your holy place, which I previously would never dare enter because I was stained with sin. Thank you for restoring my life and inviting me into your presence.

Have you experienced the power of restoration in your life?

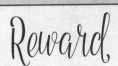

Reward

Work willingly at whatever you do, as though you were
working for the Lord rather than for people. Remember
that the Lord will give you an inheritance as your reward,
and that the Master you are serving is Christ.

COLOSSIANS 3:23-24 NLT

"Love your enemies, do good to them, and lend to them
without expecting to get anything back. Then your
reward will be great, and you will be children of the Most
High, because he is kind to the ungrateful and wicked."

LUKE 6:35 NIV

Without faith living within us it would be impossible to
please God. For we come to God in faith knowing that he
is real and that he rewards the faith of those who give all
their passion and strength into seeking him.

HEBREWS 11:6 TPT

God, your Word says that you are kind to people even when they are ungrateful and wicked. Help me to be like you, even when my diligent attempts seem to go unnoticed or unappreciated. You even promise to reward my diligence and my faith.

When coworkers, family, or friends are difficult, I can remember that it is really you who I am serving. When all my hard work goes unacknowledged, I remember that you are my reward.

How does it make you feel knowing that God will reward you for your diligence?

Safety

The LORD also will be a refuge for the oppressed,
A refuge in times of trouble.
Those who know Your name will put their trust in You;
For You, LORD, have not forsaken those who seek You.

PSALM 9:9–10 NKJV

The name of the LORD is a strong tower;
The righteous runs into it and is safe.

PROVERBS 18:10 NASB

Wherever I am, though far away at the ends of the earth,
I will cry to you for help. When my heart is faint and
overwhelmed, lead me to the mighty, towering Rock of
safety. For you are my refuge, a high tower where my
enemies can never reach me.

PSALM 61:2-3 TLB

Fear has no voice next to you. I know that when I am with you, I am safe. Like a good parent, you provide safety for me from my enemies and assurance that I am never alone.

In times of trouble, you are right there guarding me. When nobody else is around to help me, you are beside me ready to guide me. Thank you for always keeping me safe and close to you.

Do you feel safe when you think about God being near you?

Salvation

"This is how God loved the world: He gave his one and only Son, so that everyone who believes in him will not perish but have eternal life."

John 3:16 NLT

The wages of sin is death, but the gift of God is eternal life in Christ Jesus our Lord.

Romans 6:23 NIV

God's grace has saved you because of your faith in Christ. Your salvation doesn't come from anything you do. It is God's gift.

Ephesians 2:8 NIRV

If you openly declare that Jesus is Lord and believe in your heart that God raised him from the dead, you will be saved.

Romans 10:9 NLT

There was a time when I had no hope for the future because I had sinned and could not approach you. I did not qualify for entrance into your Kingdom because I was imperfect and couldn't bring my filth into perfection.

Darkness does not approach the light. You saw me in the wretched state I was in, loved me, and offered me salvation by paying for my sins yourself. Your salvation is the greatest gift I have ever received! Thank you.

How do you respond to the message of salvation?

Satisfaction

Because your love is better than life,
my lips will glorify you.
I will praise you as long as I live,
and in your name I will lift up my hands.
I will be fully satisfied as with the richest of foods;
with singing lips my mouth will praise you.

PSALM 63:3–5 NIV

"Give, and it will be given to you. A good measure,
pressed down, shaken together and running over, will
be poured into your lap. For with the measure you use, it
will be measured to you."

LUKE 6:38 NIV

Whoever pursues righteousness and love
finds life, prosperity and honor.

PROVERBS 21:21 NIV

Every day I am bombarded by myriads of messages telling me what I need in order to feel satisfied. Then I open your Word and read the truth about the satisfaction you bring.

Knowing you and being loved by you is so much more satisfying than food or riches or even any other relationships. In you, I find everything I need and all that I desire.

Are you satisfied with all God
has given you?

Strength

God is our refuge and strength,
an ever-present help in trouble.

PSALM 46:1 NIV

The Lord is faithful; he will strengthen you
and guard you from the evil one.

2 THESSALONIANS 3:3 NIRV

Don't be afraid, for I am with you.
Don't be discouraged, for I am your God.
I will strengthen you and help you.
I will hold you up with my victorious right hand.

ISAIAH 41:10 NLT

Just as you gave David strength to conquer Goliath, please give me the strength to stand up against anything that defies you. There are a lot of evil forces that I am not strong enough to defeat, but you are.

There is nothing that can stand up against you, and you have put your strength in me. When I feel weak and insignificant, you take me by the hand and lead me into victory. I will not be discouraged because I know you are faithful.

What makes you feel strong?

Stress

Praise the LORD, my soul;
all my inmost being, praise his holy name.
Praise the LORD, my soul,
and forget not all his benefits—
who forgives all your sins
and heals all your diseases,
who redeems your life from the pit
and crowns you with love and compassion,
who satisfies your desires with good things
so that your youth is renewed like the eagle's.

PSALM 103:1-5 NIV

Commit your actions to the LORD.
and your plans will succeed.

PROVERBS 16:3 NLT

As soon as the aim of my day becomes about me and my accomplishments, stress is invited in. Stress is needless if I have truly committed my plans and their results to you because you will be the one who allows them to succeed or fail. I can till, plant, and water all day, but only you can cause a plant to grow.

Sometimes I lose sight and get caught up chasing my end goals, then I succumb to consequential stressful situations. Help me remember that you bring the increase and I can trust you with the results.

When was the last time you were able
to let go of stress and just sit with God?

Support

Whom have I in heaven but you?
And earth has nothing I desire besides you.
My flesh and my heart may fail,
but God is the strength of my heart
and my portion forever.

<small>PSALM 73:25–26 NIV</small>

The LORD is near to the brokenhearted
and saves the crushed in spirit.

<small>PSALM 34:18 ESV</small>

You, God, see the trouble of the afflicted;
you consider their grief and take it in hand.
The victims commit themselves to you;
you are the helper of the fatherless.

<small>PSALM 10:14 NIV</small>

Sometimes my grief becomes too much to bear, and too much for others to bear as well. I feel as if the weight of it will crush me. Those are the moments when you intervene and offer me support. Your Word says that you are near to the brokenhearted, you see the afflicted, you are the helper of the fatherless, and you will never forget the needy. You are not overwhelmed or disinterested in my anguish. In fact, it is where you dwell!

My problems are not too big for you. You have taken my grief in your hand and have offered me a hiding place in you. You have given me hope.

When do you feel most supported by God?

Sustenance

God is able to bless you abundantly, so that in all things
at all times, having all that you need, you will abound in
every good work.

2 Corinthians 9:8 NIV

I fall to my knees and pray to the Father, the Creator of
everything in heaven and on earth. I pray that from his
glorious, unlimited resources he will empower you with
inner strength through his Spirit. Then Christ will make
his home in your hearts as you trust in him. Your roots
will grow down into God's love and keep you strong.
And may you have the power to understand, as all God's
people should, how wide, how long, how high, and how
deep his love is. May you experience the love of Christ,
though it is too great to understand fully. Then you will
be made complete with all the fullness of life and power
that comes from God.

Ephesians 3:14–19 NLT

Because of you, I lack nothing. You sustain me with your goodness. You have blessed me richly and I have everything I need. Your limitless love is beyond my comprehension and is enough to sustain me through anything. The sustenance you offer restores my soul and reminds me that you are in control.

As I spend time with you, I am filled with your love. My strength returns and my mind is at peace again.

How do you get your sustenance from God?

Trust

May everyone who knows your mercy
keep putting their trust in you,
for they can count on you for help no matter what.
O Lord, you will never, no never,
neglect those who come to you.

Psalm 9:10 TPT

I trust in you, Lord. I say, "You are my God."
My whole life is in your hands.
Save me from the hands of my enemies.
Save me from those who are chasing me.

Psalm 31:14-15 NIRV

Yes, the Lord is for me; he will help me.
I will look in triumph at those who hate me.
It is better to take refuge in the Lord
than to trust in people.

Psalm 118:7-8 NLT

My confidence in you, Lord, is rooted in your proven goodness and faithfulness stretched across all of history. Never in all of time has there been a more trustworthy testimony. You did not have to prove yourself to me, but you did and you continue to.

Whenever I call on you, you answer. If I am faced with a problem, you help me navigate it. In the instances you ask me to step out in faith and trust you, I always find myself safely guarded by you the whole way through. I know I can securely put my trust in you.

How do you know that God is trustworthy?

Truth

"When he, the Spirit of truth, comes,
he will guide you into all the truth."

JOHN 16:13 NIV

The very essence of your words is truth;
all your just regulations will stand forever.

PSALM 119:160 NLT

"If you abide in My word,
you are My disciples indeed.
And you shall know the truth,
and the truth shall make you free."

JOHN 8:31–32 NKJV

Teach me your way, O LORD, that I may walk in your truth;
unite my heart to fear your name.

PSALM 86:11 ESV

God, you are the Spirit of truth, and if I am your child then I am also a child of truth. When faced with the temptation to be dishonest, I will remember that it is by your truth that I am set free and that I am your disciple. Help me to live honestly in the light.

I pray that I learn to fear you more than the consequences of telling the truth. Your truth will always reign supreme and I want to walk in the same way you do.

What steps can you take to be more truthful in your everyday life?

Understanding

Understanding is like a fountain of life
to those who have it.
But foolish people are punished
for the foolish things they do.

PROVERBS 16:22 NIRV

The teaching of your word gives light,
so even the simple can understand.

PSALM 119:130 NLT

Give me understanding,
so that I may keep your law
and obey it with all my heart.

PSALM 119:34 NIV

Don't act thoughtlessly,
but understand what the Lord wants you to do.

EPHESIANS 5:17 NLT

God, rather than acting foolishly in ignorance, help me to understand. I pray that every day I will grow in understanding as I read your teachings and keep your Word in my heart. Show me what you want me to do so I don't flippantly wander through life.

Help me understand your laws so I obey them. I do not need to be a scholar to follow you because your Word says even the simple can understand it. I will retain what I have learned so I can live for you and share it with others.

How do you seek to understand God's will each day?

Victory

You can prepare a horse for the day of battle.
But the power to win comes from the LORD.

PROVERBS 21:31 NIRV

Every child of God defeats this evil world,
and we achieve this victory through our faith.

1 JOHN 5:4 NLT

From the LORD comes deliverance.
May your blessing be on your people.

PSALM 3:8 NIV

"The LORD your God is the one who goes with you to fight
for you against your enemies to give you victory."

DEUTERONOMY 20:4 NIV

As a mighty leader and an omnipotent God, you have already promised me victory over death. The end of my story concludes in triumph and an everlasting life with you. You have defeated the world and, so, I defeat it by having faith in you.

As I address the present battles faced every day, I can have confidence knowing that you go with me and will help me emerge victorious. The power to overcome is found in you alone.

You win with Jesus in your life! Can you think of the last victory you experienced?

Wholeness

He will take our weak mortal bodies and change them
into glorious bodies like his own, using the same power
with which he will bring everything under his control.

Celebrate with praises the God and Father of our Lord
Jesus Christ, who has shown us his extravagant mercy.
For his fountain of mercy has given us a new life—we are
reborn to experience a living, energetic hope through
the resurrection of Jesus Christ from the dead. We are
reborn into a perfect inheritance that can never perish,
never be defiled, and never diminish. It is promised
and preserved forever in the heavenly realm for you!
Through our faith, the mighty power of God constantly
guards us until our full salvation is ready to be revealed
in the last time.

1 PETER 1:3–5 TPT

God, my body is breaking down and I recognize this every day.
Thank you that my hope is not in myself or my mortal body.
Thank you that you bring healing and wholeness. Your mercy
grants me new life and one day I will be reborn.

This life and all of its splendors will break down and perish,
but within the new life that you offer I will experience what
it is like to truly be whole. This is the reality that will
remain forever.

How does understanding eternal wholeness
benefit you in this life?

Wisdom

Wisdom will come into your mind,
and knowledge will be pleasing to you.
Good sense will protect you;
understanding will guard you
It will keep you from the wicked,
from those whose words are bad.

PROVERBS 2:10-12 NCV

Wisdom and money can get you almost anything,
but only wisdom can save your life.

ECCLESIASTES 7:12 NLT

If any of you needs wisdom, you should ask God for it.
He will give it to you. God gives freely to everyone and
doesn't find fault.

JAMES 1:5 NIRV

The wisdom which comes from you will protect me from following foolish whims and ideas. When others set traps for me and try to get me to fall, wisdom will save me from the snares.

Your wisdom is far superior to knowledge or money because it is true understanding that you have given me. If I ever need wisdom, you freely give it when I ask you for it. Please continue to help me make wise choices as I follow you.

How can you use God's wisdom to make better choices?

BroadStreet Publishing Group, LLC.
Savage, Minnesota USA
Broadstreetpublishing.com

Prayers & Promises for Comfort and Encouragement

© 2019 by BroadStreet Publishing
978-1-4245-5917-6 (faux)
978-1-4245-5918-3 (ebook)

Prayers composed by Brenna Stockman.

Design by Chris Garborg | garborgdesign.com
Compiled and edited by Michelle Winger | literallyprecise.com

Printed in China.

19 20 21 22 23 24 25 7 6 5 4 3 2 1